THE ROYAL HORTICULTURAL SOCIETY

WILD IN THE GARDEN

DIARY
2022

Inspiring everyone to grow

First published in 2021 by Frances Lincoln Publishing,
an imprint of The Quarto Group.
The Old Brewery, 6 Blundell Street
London, N7 9BH, United Kingdom
www.QuartoKnows.com

Astronomical information © Crown Copyright
Reproduced by permission of HMNAO, UKHO and the
Controller of Her Majesty's Stationery Office.

ISBN 978 0 7112 6222 5

10 9 8 7 6 5 4 3 2 1

Design by Sarah Pyke

Printed in China

RHS FLOWER SHOWS 2022

The Royal Horticultural Society holds a number of
prestigious flower shows throughout the year. At the
time of going to press, show dates for 2022 had not been
confirmed but details can be found on the website at:
rhs.org.uk/shows-events

Every effort is made to ensure calendarial data is correct
at the time of going to press but the publisher cannot
accept any liability for any errors or changes.

Front cover: European hedgehog (*Erinaceus europaeus*)
Back cover: European robin (*Erithacus rubecula*)

PICTURE CREDITS

CALENDAR 2022

JANUARY

M	T	W	T	F	S	S
					1	2
3	4	5	6	7	8	9
10	11	12	13	14	15	16
17	18	19	20	21	22	23
24	25	26	27	28	29	30
31						

FEBRUARY

M	T	W	T	F	S	S
	1	2	3	4	5	6
7	8	9	10	11	12	13
14	15	16	17	18	19	20
21	22	23	24	25	26	27
28						

MARCH

M	T	W	T	F	S	S
	1	2	3	4	5	6
7	8	9	10	11	12	13
14	15	16	17	18	19	20
21	22	23	24	25	26	27
28	29	30	31			

APRIL

M	T	W	T	F	S	S
				1	2	3
4	5	6	7	8	9	10
11	12	13	14	15	16	17
18	19	20	21	22	23	24
25	26	27	28	29	30	

MAY

M	T	W	T	F	S	S
						1
2	3	4	5	6	7	8
9	10	11	12	13	14	15
16	17	18	19	20	21	22
23	24	25	26	27	28	29
30	31					

JUNE

M	T	W	T	F	S	S
	1	2	3	4	5	
6	7	8	9	10	11	12
13	14	15	16	17	18	19
20	21	22	23	24	25	26
27	28	29	30			

JULY

M	T	W	T	F	S	S
				1	2	3
4	5	6	7	8	9	10
11	12	13	14	15	16	17
18	19	20	21	22	23	24
25	26	27	28	29	30	31

AUGUST

M	T	W	T	F	S	S
1	2	3	4	5	6	7
8	9	10	11	12	13	14
15	16	17	18	19	20	21
22	23	24	25	26	27	28
29	30	31				

SEPTEMBER

M	T	W	T	F	S	S
			1	2	3	4
5	6	7	8	9	10	11
12	13	14	15	16	17	18
19	20	21	22	23	24	25
26	27	28	29	30		

OCTOBER

M	T	W	T	F	S	S
					1	2
3	4	5	6	7	8	9
10	11	12	13	14	15	16
17	18	19	20	21	22	23
24	25	26	27	28	29	30
31						

NOVEMBER

M	T	W	T	F	S	S
	1	2	3	4	5	6
7	8	9	10	11	12	13
14	15	16	17	18	19	20
21	22	23	24	25	26	27
28	29	30				

DECEMBER

M	T	W	T	F	S	S
			1	2	3	4
5	6	7	8	9	10	11
12	13	14	15	16	17	18
19	20	21	22	23	24	25
26	27	28	29	30	31	

CALENDAR 2023

JANUARY

M	T	W	T	F	S	S
						1
2	3	4	5	6	7	8
9	10	11	12	13	14	15
16	17	18	19	20	21	22
23	24	25	26	27	28	29
30	31					

FEBRUARY

M	T	W	T	F	S	S
		1	2	3	4	5
6	7	8	9	10	11	12
13	14	15	16	17	18	19
20	21	22	23	24	25	26
27	28					

MARCH

M	T	W	T	F	S	S
		1	2	3	4	5
6	7	8	9	10	11	12
13	14	15	16	17	18	19
20	21	22	23	24	25	26
27	28	29	30	31		

APRIL

M	T	W	T	F	S	S
					1	2
3	4	5	6	7	8	9
10	11	12	13	14	15	16
17	18	19	20	21	22	23
24	25	26	27	28	29	30

MAY

M	T	W	T	F	S	S
1	2	3	4	5	6	7
8	9	10	11	12	13	14
15	16	17	18	19	20	21
22	23	24	25	26	27	28
29	30	31				

JUNE

M	T	W	T	F	S	S
			1	2	3	4
5	6	7	8	9	10	11
12	13	14	15	16	17	18
19	20	21	22	23	24	25
26	27	28	29	30		

JULY

M	T	W	T	F	S	S
					1	2
3	4	5	6	7	8	9
10	11	12	13	14	15	16
17	18	19	20	21	22	23
24	25	26	27	28	29	30
31						

AUGUST

M	T	W	T	F	S	S
1	2	3	4	5	6	
7	8	9	10	11	12	13
14	15	16	17	18	10	20
21	22	23	24	25	26	27
28	29	30	31			

SEPTEMBER

M	T	W	T	F	S	S
				1	2	3
4	5	6	7	8	9	10
11	12	13	14	15	16	17
18	19	20	21	22	23	24
25	26	27	28	29	30	

OCTOBER

M	T	W	T	F	S	S
						1
2	3	4	5	6	7	8
9	10	11	12	13	14	15
16	17	18	19	20	21	22
23	24	25	26	27	28	29
30	31					

NOVEMBER

M	T	W	T	F	S	S
		1	2	3	4	5
6	7	8	9	10	11	12
13	14	15	16	17	18	19
20	21	22	23	24	25	26
27	28	29	30			

DECEMBER

M	T	W	T	F	S	S
				1	2	3
4	5	6	7	8	9	10
11	12	13	14	15	16	17
18	19	20	21	22	23	24
25	26	27	28	29	30	31

GARDENS AND WILDLIFE

Gardens are an important ecosystem. All ecosystems are interdependent and dynamic systems of living organisms interacting with the physical environment. Gardens by their very nature are extremely variable, with a diversity of plants that can surpass that of 'natural' ecosystems. Combined with resources such as ponds and compost heaps, gardens deliver a wide variety of habitats where wildlife can thrive. Gardens provide food and a home for hundreds of creatures throughout their lifecycles, and this wildlife is vital to a healthy and vibrant living garden.

The large range of garden wildlife is there because of gardening, not despite it. Gardens provide resources year-round, from overwintering sites to summer food plants. No garden or green space is too small to provide some benefit. A window box, for instance, can provide a nectar stop for a bumblebees and other pollinators. The huge range of plants and variety of garden management results in a mosaic of habitats spanning a much wider area than a single garden. Wildlife doesn't recognise our boundaries and gardens provide important corridors facilitating the movement of mammals such as hedgehogs, birds, butterflies and other creatures.

Most gardens already support a variety of wildlife and with a little thought and planning they can do even more. Adding more plants, and perhaps a pond, bird, bee and bat boxes, decaying wood, a compost heap or an undisturbed leaf pile will provide valuable habitats. The more diverse the habitats, the greater the number of species of birds, bees, bats, beetles, moths and other wildlife that will use a garden. The RHS recognises and actively promotes the valuable contribution that wildlife makes to gardens and gardens to wildlife. The act of gardening for wildlife can also bring great enjoyment and health benefits to gardeners. For more information visit: www.rhs.org.uk and www.wildaboutgardens.org

Common blue butterfly *(Polyommatus icarus)*

JOBS FOR THE MONTH

- Clean the bird bath and feeding stations regularly to help prevent diseases, and make sure that the water is kept topped up.
- Ensure there is accessible water that has not frozen over, as this is essential for drinking and bathing. Make sure ponds have sloping edges or a ramp so wildlife can climb out if necessary.
- Put bird food on the ground, bird table and in bird feeders.

INSECTS

- Insects and other invertebrates are crucial to the natural balance of your garden. Many are vital in nutrient recycling, helping break down dead plant matter, while others are predatory, helping balance those that feed on plants. Many flying insects are pollinators.
- Wildlife will use all areas of your garden but in a small or busy space you may want to identify a patch where the grass is allowed to grow long or where disturbance is kept to a minimum, such as behind a shed.
- Evergreen bushes and climbers, fallen leaves, dead stems and seed heads provide winter shelter for many insects.

'Try to keep your feeding regime consistent to encourage birds to regularly return to the garden'

BIRDS

- Blackbirds, blackcaps, tits, thrushes and robins are all common birds to see in winter. Look out for redwings and fieldfares too.
- Many natural food sources, such as seeds and berries, are exhausted by this time in winter, so feeding garden birds is more important than ever.
- Buy high quality bird food from online or retail outlets, or make your own fat balls using natural fats such as lard and beef suet. Fat from cooking and unsaturated margarines and vegetable oil are not suitable.
- If possible, try to keep your feeding regime consistent to encourage birds to regularly return to the garden.
- Protect birds from predators by siting bird feeders away from areas easily accessible to cats.

DECEMBER & JANUARY

Monday **27**

Tuesday **28**

Wednesday **29**

Thursday **30**

New Year's Eve   *Friday* **31**

New Year's Day   *Saturday* **1**

New moon   *Sunday* **2**

JANUARY

3 *Monday*

Holiday, UK, Republic of Ireland, USA, Canada,
Australia and New Zealand (New Year's Day)

4 *Tuesday*

Holiday, Scotland and New Zealand

5 *Wednesday*

6 *Thursday*

Epiphany

7 *Friday*

8 *Saturday*

9 *Sunday*

First quarter

Great tit *(Parus major)*

JANUARY

Monday 10

Tuesday 11

Wednesday 12

Thursday 13

Friday 14

Saturday 15

Sunday 16

Common frog *(Rana temporaria)*

JANUARY

---

17 *Monday*

Full moon
Holiday, USA (Martin Luther King Jnr Day)

---

18 *Tuesday*

---

19 *Wednesday*

---

20 *Thursday*

---

21 *Friday*

---

22 *Saturday*

---

23 *Sunday*

JANUARY

Monday **24**

Last quarter

Tuesday **25**

Holiday, Australia (Australia Day)

Wednesday **26**

Thursday **27**

Friday **28**

Saturday **29**

Sunday **30**

Fallow deer *(Dama dama)*

JANUARY & FEBRUARY

31 *Monday*

1 *Tuesday*

New moon
Chinese New Year

2 *Wednesday*

3 *Thursday*

4 *Friday*

5 *Saturday*

6 *Sunday*

Accession of Queen Elizabeth II
Waitangi Day (New Zealand)

'Make sure the bird bath and table are kept clear of ice'

JOBS FOR THE MONTH

- Continue to put food out on the ground and keep bird feeders topped up. Move the feeding station around every few weeks so spilt food doesn't build up (this can encourage less desirable visitors such as rats, and can lead to the spread of avian diseases). It also helps to avoid putting out large chunks of food.
- Put up nest boxes for birds.
- If possible, keep the bird bath topped up and ice-free, as birds still need to bathe regardless of the cold.

HABITATS AND SHELTER

- Now is the time to consider building or buying a bee home for solitary or mason bees to colonise in the spring.
- Hang nest boxes 1-3m high on walls or trees and fit metal nest-box plates to protect birds from predators such as grey squirrels and jays. Tilt the box forward slightly to reduce splash from rain showers.
- Make sure nest boxes face between north and east, as the heat from sunlight can make a nest box uninviting.
- A pile of old logs or bricks can provide welcome shelter for insects and other small creatures.

PONDS

A pond is a great way to encourage a variety of wildlife into your garden. Even the smallest pond will attract birds, insects, newts, toads and frogs, while also providing an important water source.

BUILDING A POND

- Late winter is a great time to put in a pond. You may get your first frogs and toads by spring.
- Choose a bright, sunny location with at least one sloping side to provide easy access in and out of the water.
- Try to vary the depth of the water, so there are shallow parts as well as deeper areas.
- Connect your water butt to the pond to automatically fill it during heavy rain.
- Include a section at the pond margin with gravel or stones to provide easy drinking spots for bees and other pollinators.
- Try planting vegetation around the edges of the pond or letting grass grow long to create a safe passage for animals such as froglets to enter and exit the pond.

FEBRUARY

Holiday, New Zealand (Waitangi Day)

Monday **7**

First quarter

Tuesday **8**

Wednesday **9**

Thursday **10**

Friday **11**

Saturday **12**

Sunday **13**

Common blackbird *(Turdus merula)*

FEBRUARY

14 *Monday*   Valentine's Day

15 *Tuesday*

16 *Wednesday*   *Full moon*

17 *Thursday*

18 *Friday*

19 *Saturday*

20 *Sunday*

Seven-spot ladybird *(Coccinella septempunctata)* in a lavender field

FEBRUARY

Holiday, USA (Presidents' Day)

Monday 21

Tuesday 22

quarter

Wednesday 23

Thursday 24

Friday 25

Saturday 26

Sunday 27

Common blue damselfly *(Enallagma cyathigerum)*

FEBRUARY & MARCH

28 *Monday*

1 *Tuesday*   St David's Day
                                                                 Shrove Tuesday

2 *Wednesday*   *New moon*
                                                                 Ash Wednesday

3 *Thursday*

4 *Friday*

5 *Saturday*

6 *Sunday*

'Remember to leave some 'weeds' in lawns, such as dandelions which are a valuable source of nectar and pollen'

JOBS FOR THE MONTH

Provide shelter for wildlife by creating a log pile or 'dead hedge' using woody prunings.
- Continue to clean out and top up bird feeders. Place whole peanuts in a metal mesh feeder to avoid a choking hazard for young birds.
- Put out hedgehog food and check for hazards such as loose netting and uncovered drains.
- Keep the bird bath topped up and clean it regularly.
- Make your pond more wildlife friendly (see Week 5).
- Sow or plant a wildflower meadow.

AMPHIBIANS

- As the weather warms up, frogs and toads emerge from overwintering sites.
- Look out for amphibian spawn in ponds. Frog spawn is usually in jelly-like clumps; toad spawn is in longer individual strands; and newt spawn is laid individually on pondweed stems.

WAYS TO ENCOURAGE WILDLIFE

- Build a compost heap to recycle garden waste and provide habitat for a wide range of wildlife.
- Replacing a fence with a mixed hedge will provide a safe 'corridor' for wildlife to move along, as well as an overwintering and nesting site and food source for small mammals, birds and some species of bumblebee.
- Encourage ground-feeding birds such as robins and dunnocks by placing food on wire mesh positioned just off the ground.
- Weed by hand as much as possible to avoid using herbicides but remember to leave some 'weeds' in lawns, such as dandelions which are a valuable source of nectar and pollen.
- Favour plants known to support wildlife; honeysuckle, hawthorn, pyracantha, sunflower and rowan trees are all popular with a range of wildlife.
- Mulch beds with garden compost or composted bark to help feed earthworms and maintain a healthy living soil.

MARCH

Monday **7**

Tuesday **8**

Wednesday **9**

First quarter

Thursday **10**

Friday **11**

Saturday **12**

Sunday **13**

Common toad *(Bufo bufo)*

MARCH

14 *Monday*   Commonwealth Day

15 *Tuesday*

16 *Wednesday*

17 *Thursday*

St Patrick's Day
Holiday, Republic of Ireland and Northern Ireland

18 *Friday*   *Full moon*

19 *Saturday*

20 *Sunday*   Vernal Equinox (Spring begins)

Eurasian siskin *(Spinus spinus)*

MARCH

Monday **21**

Tuesday **22**

Wednesday **23**

Thursday **24**

ast quarter

Friday **25**

Saturday **26**

othering Sunday, UK and Republic of Ireland
ritish Summer Time begins

Sunday **27**

arden spider *(Araneus diadematus)*

---

28 *Monday*

---

29 *Tuesday*

---

30 *Wednesday*

---

31 *Thursday*

---

1 *Friday*   *New moon*

---

2 *Saturday*

---

3 *Sunday*   First day of Ramadân (subject to sighting of the moon)

A wildflower field featuring scented mayweed *(Matricaria recutita)* and a common poppy *(Papaver rhoeas)*

JOBS FOR THE MONTH

- Plant annuals and perennials (single flowers as opposed to double flowers) to encourage pollinators into the garden. Look for these on the RHS Plants for Pollinators list.
- Plant up a hanging basket or windowbox for bees and butterflies using nasturtiums, English marigolds and lavender. Position somewhere sunny.
- Stop mowing an area of lawn to allow the grass and flowers to grow. This will attract all sorts of grasshoppers, bugs, ground-nesting bees and other insects.
- Keep the bird bath and bird feeders clean and topped up.
- Leave out food for hedgehogs.

CHOOSING A BIRD TABLE

A bird table can be a simple tray, with or without a roof. A raised edge will retain food and a gap in each corner will allow water to drain away and facilitate cleaning. It is best to avoid fancy designs as these can be difficult to clean. Choose a location out of reach of predators such as cats.

'Bats are a good indication of a healthy, insect-rich environment'

BATS

- Bats are a good indication of a healthy, insect-rich environment.
- Now is the time that bats begin to move to maternity roosts, so it would be a good time to make or buy a bat box and mount it as high as possible on a sunny wall. Avoid positions close to security lights and keep garden lighting to a minimum.
- Other common roosting sites include eaves or behind weatherboarding on the south face of buildings.
- There are 17 species of bat that breed in Britain but their numbers have declined. The more common species likely to be seen in the garden are the common pipistrelle, soprano pipistrelle, brown long-eared, noctule and Daubenton's.
- Bats eat flying insects at night, including mosquitoes, moths and beetles, and so help keep a natural balance. Bats add life to a garden in the evening.
- Garden ponds and night-flowering plants such as evening primrose encourage the types of insects that bats like to eat.

APRIL

Monday **4**

Tuesday **5**

Wednesday **6**

Thursday **7**

Friday **8**

First quarter

Saturday **9**

Palm Sunday

Sunday **10**

APRIL

11 *Monday*

12 *Tuesday*

13 *Wednesday*

14 *Thursday*

Maundy Thursday

15 *Friday*

Good Friday
Holiday, UK, Canada, Australia and New Zealand

16 *Saturday*

Full moon
First day of Passover (Pesach)

17 *Sunday*

Easter Sunday

Bank vole *(Myodes glareolus)*

APRIL

Easter Monday
Holiday, UK (exc. Scotland), Republic of Ireland,
Australia and New Zealand

Monday **18**

Tuesday **19**

Wednesday **20**

Birthday of Queen Elizabeth II

Thursday **21**

Friday **22**

Last quarter
St George's Day

Saturday **23**

Sunday **24**

Spring flowering blossom on an apple tree *(Malus domestica)*

APRIL & MAY

25 *Monday*   Holiday, Australia and New Zealand (Anzac Day)

26 *Tuesday*

27 *Wednesday*

28 *Thursday*

29 *Friday*

30 *Saturday*   *New moon*

1 *Sunday*

JOBS FOR THE MONTH

- Remove excess plant growth from ponds, leaving it on the side for twenty-four hours to allow any trapped creatures to return to the water before adding it to the compost heap.
- Sow annuals such as cosmos, phacelia and cornflower to attract insects.
- Be careful to avoid disturbing birds' nests in boxes, shrubs and hedges.
- Regularly top up and clean out the bird bath and feeders.
- Leave informal hedges untrimmed to provide food and shelter for wildlife.
- Continue to top up bird feeders but stop feeding for six weeks if you spot any sick birds.
- Mow a path through any areas of long grass and pull out any weeds in areas sown with cornfield annuals or other annual flower mixes.
- Allow some of your plants to go to seed.

BIRDS

- By this time in the year, migrant birds such as swifts and swallows from Africa have arrived.
- The dawn chorus can be deafening as birds compete for territories and mates.

'Choose annuals and perennials to attract insects'

MAKE A WILDLIFE CONTAINER POND

Repurpose an old Belfast sink or plastic container to make a wildlife-friendly container pond.

1. Position your container somewhere you can enjoy, ideally with a little sun – but not for the whole day, as the water can warm up too much or evaporate too quickly.
2. If the container leaks, use a sheet of pond liner to make it watertight, securing it in place with a silicone-based sealer.
3. Make it wildlife friendly by creating a ramp so that frogs and other wildlife can get in and out. A stack of stones, bricks, logs or a plank of untreated wood covered in chickenwire for little legs to grip onto all work well.
4. Fill it with rainwater.
5. Gently lower in a mix of floating and upright pond plants. Three to five plants is usually enough for a mini-pond – they may look small at first, but they can grow very quickly.

MAY

Early Spring Bank Holiday, UK
Holiday, Republic of Ireland

Monday 2

Eid al-Fitr (end of Ramadân)
(subject to sighting of the moon)

Tuesday 3

Wednesday 4

Thursday 5

Friday 6

Saturday 7

Mother's Day, USA, Canada, Australia and New Zealand

Sunday 8

Comma butterfly *(Polygonia c-album)*

MAY

9 *Monday*   *First quarter*

10 *Tuesday*

11 *Wednesday*

12 *Thursday*

13 *Friday*

14 *Saturday*

15 *Sunday*

European rabbit *(Oryctolagus cuniculus)*

MAY

Full moon   *Monday* **16**

Tuesday **17**

Wednesday **18**

Thursday **19**

Friday **20**

Saturday **21**

Last quarter   *Sunday* **22**

A bumblebee *(Bombus)* sitting on a seaside daisy *(Erigeron glaucous* 'Sea breeze')

MAY

---

23 *Monday*   Holiday, Canada (Victoria Day)

---

24 *Tuesday*

---

25 *Wednesday*

---

26 *Thursday*   Ascension Day

---

27 *Friday*

---

28 *Saturday*

---

29 *Sunday*

Red squirrel *(Sciurus vulgaris)*

JOBS FOR THE MONTH

- Thin out or cut back excessive new growth on aquatic plants. Leave by the side of the pond for a while before transferring to the compost heap.
- Mow spring-flowering meadows once bulb foliage has died down.
- Control unwanted plants and encourage good root establishment by mowing recently established perennial meadows every six to eight weeks.
- Allow herbs such as marjoram, mint and sage to flower to encourage bees and butterflies.
- Grow plants bigger before planting out and use biological slug control if necessary.
- Make a 'bee drinker' out of a plant saucer filled with pebbles and water.
- Allow your lawn to grow longer by letting some flowers bloom and avoiding the use of weedkillers. This will allow insect life to thrive.

'Many creatures give birth to and are raising young around this time of year'

CHOOSING BIRD FOOD

If you want to encourage a particular species of bird into your garden, try leaving out their favourite food.

- **Dunnocks** fat and small seeds on the ground
- **Robins** live mealworms
- **Starlings** peanut cakes
- **Finches** berry cakes
- **Goldfinches** niger seeds
- **Sparrows, finches and nuthatches** sunflower heads
- **Tits** insect cakes
- **Wrens** prefer natural foods but will take fat and seed
- **Thrushes and blackbirds** fruit such as over-ripe apples, raisins and songbird mix scattered on the ground

HEDGEHOGS

Many creatures are raising young at this time of year. Hedgehogs in particular are very active, and if you are lucky you may see or hear them foraging for food at night.

MAY & JUNE

New moon
Holiday, USA (Memorial Day)

Monday **30**

Tuesday **31**

Wednesday **1**

Spring Bank Holiday, UK
Coronation Day

Thursday **2**

Bank Holiday, UK (Queen's Platinum Jubilee)

Friday **3**

Saturday **4**

Feast of Weeks (Shavuot)
Whit Sunday

Sunday **5**

JUNE

---

6 *Monday*

Holiday, Republic of Ireland
Holiday, New Zealand (The Queen's Birthday)

---

7 *Tuesday*

First quarter

---

8 *Wednesday*

---

9 *Thursday*

---

10 *Friday*

---

11 *Saturday*

The Queen's Official Birthday (subject to confirmation)

---

12 *Sunday*

Trinity Sunday

Orange-tip butterfly *(Anthocharis cardamines)*

Holiday, Australia (The Queen's Birthday)   *Monday* **13**

Full moon   *Tuesday* **14**

Wednesday **15**

Corpus Christi   *Thursday* **16**

Friday **17**

Saturday **18**

Father's Day, UK, Republic of Ireland, USA and Canada   *Sunday* **19**

Chaffinch *(Fringilla coelebs)*

JUNE

---

20 *Monday*

---

21 *Tuesday*

Last quarter
Summer Solstice (Summer begins)

---

22 *Wednesday*

---

23 *Thursday*

---

24 *Friday*

---

25 *Saturday*

---

26 *Sunday*

Buff-tailed bumblebee *(Bombus terrestris)* on a lavender flower

'Delay hedge trimming until the end of summer to allow wildlife to nest, shelter and feed in them'

JOBS FOR THE MONTH

- Top up ponds and water features if necessary, ideally using stored rainwater.
- Remove dead foliage and blooms from water lilies and other aquatic plants. Leave at the side of the pond for a while to allow wildlife to return to the water.
- Plant annuals and perennials to attract insects.
- Avoid deadheading roses that produce hips, as these are a valuable food source for birds in the winter months.
- Put out hedgehog food and check that any holes in the bottom of fences haven't become blocked so hedgehogs can freely move between gardens.
- Construct a hedgehog hibernation box for the coming winter.
- Leave nesting birds undisturbed in garden shrubs and trees.
- Delay hedge trimming until the end of summer to allow wildlife to nest, shelter and feed in them.
- Watch out for mating dragonflies and young frogs leaving the pond.

INSECTS

- July is the beginning of the ant mating season, so you may see lots of winged queens and males on their nuptial flights.
- Hoverflies are in abundance at this time of year. Adults are pollinators and the larvae feed on greenfly and other aphids.
- Be tolerant of plant damage and a few caterpillars and aphids to support their predators and encourage a natural balance.

BATS

All bats are legally protected in Britain, and this protection extends to their roosting and overwintering sites. During the day, bats hide in dark places like hollow trees, so retain old trees with cavities in the trunk where possible.

- This time of year is the best time for bat watching in the evening. Generally, they will seek their own spaces, but you can provide bat boxes for roosting.
- Bats are insect predators. Compost heaps and ponds will generate the type of insects bats like to eat.
- Grow plants with flowers that are likely to attract moths and other night-flying insects. White or pale coloured flowers seem to be preferred, as they are more likely to be seen by nocturnal insects.
- Avoid using pesticides.

JUNE & JULY

Monday 27

Tuesday 28

New moon

Wednesday 29

Thursday 30

Holiday, Canada (Canada Day)

Friday 1

Saturday 2

Sunday 3

JULY

---

4 *Monday*   Holiday, USA (Independence Day)

---

5 *Tuesday*

---

6 *Wednesday*

---

7 *Thursday*   *First quarter*

---

8 *Friday*

---

9 *Saturday*

---

10 *Sunday*

Wildflower meadow

JULY

Monday **11**

Battle of the Boyne
Holiday, Northern Ireland

Tuesday **12**

Full moon

Wednesday **13**

Thursday **14**

St Swithin's Day

Friday **15**

Saturday **16**

Sunday **17**

European rabbit *(Oryctolagus cuniculus)*

JULY

18 *Monday*

19 *Tuesday*

20 *Wednesday*   *Last quarter*

21 *Thursday*

22 *Friday*

23 *Saturday*

24 *Sunday*

Hawfinch *(Coccothraustes coccothraustes)*

JULY

Monday **25**

Tuesday **26**

Wednesday **27**

New moon

Thursday **28**

Friday **29**

Islamic New Year

Saturday **30**

Sunday **31**

Male beautiful demoiselle *(Calopteryx virgo)*

AUGUST

1 *Monday*   Holiday, Scotland and Republic of Ireland

2 *Tuesday*

3 *Wednesday*

4 *Thursday*

5 *Friday*   *First quarter*

6 *Saturday*

7 *Sunday*

'Spiders have an important role to play in a balanced garden – they eat many other invertebrates and can themselves be food for birds'

IN THE GARDEN
- Many adult birds fly fairly low in late summer, hiding in cool, shady places while they moult their feathers.
- Bumblebees, solitary bees and hoverflies are busy collecting nectar and pollen in the flower and herb garden. Butterflies, including the summer migrant Painted Lady, are particularly attracted to buddleja.
- Birdsong may be less obvious this month.
- In hot, dry weather many birds enjoy 'dust-bathing' as well as splashing about in the bird bath.
- Frogs and newts start to leave ponds to find new homes.

SPIDERS
- Spiders have an important role to play in a balanced garden. They eat many other invertebrates and can themselves be food for birds.
- Keep a few patches in borders that are less densely planted, as these favour hunting spiders.
- Use pesticides as little as possible.
- Plant tall plants and dense bushes to create scaffolding for spiders to build their webs on.
- Towards autumn, spiders' webs will become more visible on lawns and in borders as dew and mist droplets reveal them.

JOBS FOR THE MONTH
- Continue to top up bird feeders.
- Allow seed heads to develop on some plants as a food source. Don't trim any bushes with berries developing – such as holly, cotoneaster and pyracantha.
- Keep the bird bath and feeding stations topped up and regularly cleaned.
- Leave fledglings undisturbed if you find them on the ground – their parents are probably not far away.
- Deadhead flowers to encourage them to produce more blooms and pollen for insects.
- Sow seeds of yellow rattle into areas of long grass to help suppress excessive grass growth in favour of wildflowers.
- Leave some windfall apples, pears and plums for birds to feed on.
- Continue putting out food and water for hedgehogs.

AUGUST

Monday **8**

Tuesday **9**

Wednesday **10**

Thursday **11**

Full moon

Friday **12**

Saturday **13**

Sunday **14**

Common frog *(Rana temporaria)*

AUGUST

15 *Monday*

16 *Tuesday*

17 *Wednesday*

18 *Thursday*

19 *Friday*   *Last quarter*

20 *Saturday*

21 *Sunday*

Red fox *(Vulpes vulpes)*

AUGUST

Monday 22

Tuesday 23

Wednesday 24

Thursday 25

Friday 26

New moon

Saturday 27

Sunday 28

Small tortoiseshell *(Aglais urticae)*

AUGUST & SEPTEMBER

29 *Monday*   Summer Bank Holiday, UK (exc. Scotland)

30 *Tuesday*

31 *Wednesday*

1 *Thursday*

2 *Friday*

3 *Saturday*   *First quarter*

4 *Sunday*   Father's Day, Australia and New Zealand

JOBS FOR THE MONTH

- As we come to the end of bird nesting season, hedge trimming can resume – but delay for another month if you suspect birds are still active.
- Keep the bird bath topped up and clean regularly.
- Hedgehogs can benefit from supplementary feeding in autumn. Give them dog or cat food, never bread and milk.
- Construct a hedgehog hibernation box.
- Cover the pond surface with netting to stop excessive amounts of fallen leaves from entering.
- Give meadows a final cut before winter. Leave clippings for a couple of days to allow wildflower seeds to fall back into the meadow.
- Create piles of logs, twigs and rocks to create shelter for wildlife.

PREPARE FOR WINTER

Help overwintering creatures survive the cold weather by creating a log pile in your garden, making an insect hotel out of hollow stems or building a hedgehog box. Even a pile of old leaves left undisturbed will provide a home for small mammals and many insects. Build a hedgehog box or make piles of rocks or bricks as a place to hibernate for amphibians and other creatures.

'Hedgehogs can benefit from supplementary feeding in autumn'

BUTTERFLIES

There are 59 butterfly species that breed in Britain, plus up to 30 others that are migrant visitors from continental Europe and north Africa. In the garden, some of the most common are Red Admiral, Peacock, Brimstone, Painted Lady, Comma, Green-veined White, Small White and Large White. You may sometimes see Orange-tip, Speckled Wood, Meadow Brown, Small Copper, Holly Blue and the Small Tortoiseshell.

- Adult butterflies feed on nectar, so plant a range of nectar-rich flowers such as red valerian and asters to flower from March through to November.
- In late summer, butterflies like Red Admiral and Painted Lady will appreciate fallen fruit left on the ground.
- Many butterflies are still about in the autumn, including the Peacock, Small Tortoiseshell and Speckled Wood.
- To support butterflies, you need to look after their caterpillars, so research the plants that will best support them. For example, ivy and holly support both caterpillars and adult Holly Blue butterflies.

SEPTEMBER

Holiday, USA (Labor Day)
Holiday, Canada (Labour Day)

Monday 5

Tuesday 6

Wednesday 7

Thursday 8

Friday 9

Full moon

Saturday 10

Sunday 11

Eurasian otter (Lutra lutra)

SEPTEMBER

12 *Monday*

13 *Tuesday*

14 *Wednesday*

15 *Thursday*

16 *Friday*

17 *Saturday*

Last quarter

18 *Sunday*

European greenfinch *(Chloris chloris)*

SEPTEMBER

Monday **19**

Tuesday **20**

Wednesday **21**

Thursday **22**

Autumnal Equinox (Autumn begins)

Friday **23**

Saturday **24**

New moon

Sunday **25**

European badger *(Meles meles)*

SEPTEMBER & OCTOBER

26 *Monday*   Jewish New Year (Rosh Hashanah)

27 *Tuesday*

28 *Wednesday*

29 *Thursday*   Michaelmas Day

30 *Friday*

1 *Saturday*

2 *Sunday*

'Migrant birds start to arrive from colder, northern regions'

JOBS FOR THE MONTH

- Make a leaf pile for overwintering animals; add in some logs to widen the appeal for a greater range of insects, or build an 'insect hotel'.
- Where possible, allow uncut ivy to flower, as it is an excellent late nectar source for pollinating insects and the berries last well into winter.
- Top up bird feeders and put food out on the ground and bird tables.
- Be careful when turning over compost heaps, as frogs, toads and other small animals may be sheltering there.
- Build an 'insect hotel' using bundles of twigs or hollow stems.
- Keep the bird bath topped up and clean it regularly.
- Where possible, leave seed heads standing to provide food and shelter for wildlife.

IN THE GARDEN

- Winter migrant birds start to arrive from colder, northern regions.
- Look out for redwings, bramblings and fieldfares, but don't be surprised if your feeder is untouched. Birds will still be enjoying natural food, such as holly berries.
- Foxes are often seen in gardens searching for food so make sure to always secure your rubbish.
- Other mammals start going into overwintering sites, so put out a hedgehog hibernating box in a quiet, shady part of the garden and avoid disturbing butterflies such as Red Admirals which overwinter as adults in garden buildings.
- Many butterflies, including Small Tortoiseshell, are still about, along with hoverflies and ladybirds.
- Some moth caterpillars such as angle shades can be found feeding throughout the year. Although caterpillars eat plants, they should be tolerated when possible, as moths and butterflies form a part of a healthy balanced garden – adults are pollinators and the caterpillars vital for nesting birds.
- Food for butterfly caterpillars in gardens includes ivy, holly, hops, nasturtium, thistle, buckthorn and blackthorn.

OCTOBER

First quarter   *Monday* 3

                                                                        Tuesday 4

Day of Atonement (Yom Kippur)   *Wednesday* 5

                                                                      Thursday 6

                                                                        Friday 7

                                                                      Saturday 8

Full moon   *Sunday* 9

Eurasian harvest mouse *(Micromys minutus)*

OCTOBER

10 *Monday*

11 *Tuesday*

12 *Wednesday*

13 *Thursday*

14 *Friday*

15 *Saturday*

16 *Sunday*

Red squirrel *(Sciurus vulgaris)*

OCTOBER

Last quarter

Monday 17

Tuesday 18

Wednesday 19

Thursday 20

Friday 21

Saturday 22

Sunday 23

Song thrush *(Turdus philomelos)*

OCTOBER

---

24 *Monday*   Holiday, New Zealand (Labour Day)

---

25 *Tuesday*   *New moon*

---

26 *Wednesday*

---

27 *Thursday*

---

28 *Friday*

---

29 *Saturday*

---

30 *Sunday*   British Summer Time ends

Firethorn *(Pyracantha)*

JOBS FOR THE MONTH

- Begin to put out high-fat foods for birds such as peanut cake and fat balls.
- Make a leaf pile for hibernating mammals and retain fallen leaves at the base of hedges for blackbirds and thrushes to hunt through for tasty grubs.
- So animals still have access to water for drinking, melt a hole in ice at the edge of a pond by filling a saucepan with hot water and sitting it on the ice until a hole has melted. Never crack or hit the ice as the shock waves created can harm wildlife.
- Consider options other than a bonfire for disposing of garden waste. If you do have a bonfire always check for animals before lighting it.
- Leave seed heads standing to provide shelter and food for wildlife.
- Empty and clean out nest boxes using boiling water. When thoroughly dry, place a handful of wood shavings inside. They may provide winter shelter.
- Regularly shake off leaves from nets over ponds. Make sure other nets around the garden such as on fruit cages are now removed and safely stored away – loose nets can be a hazard to wildlife.

MOTHS

- There are over 2,500 species of moths in Britain and they play an important role in all ecosystems, including healthy gardens.
- Adult moths and their caterpillars are a key food source for various animals including hedgehogs, spiders, frogs, bats and birds. Day flying and night flying moths act as plant pollinators.
- Leave longer grasses, knapweeds and thistles in the garden, and leave hedges untrimmed if possible. Tolerate caterpillar feeding damage to plants.
- Planting evergreen shrubs will provide overwintering sites for butterflies and moths.
- Planting birch, hornbeam, hawthorn, lady's bedstraw, willow and rowan will help support moth caterpillars.
- Planting common jasmine, sweet rocket, Lychnis and sea lavender will attract day-flying moths and many other pollinators.
- Night-flowering, nectar-rich plants such as night-scented stock and pale-coloured flowering plants will attract nocturnal moths.

'Leave seed heads standing to provide shelter and food for wildlife'

OCTOBER & NOVEMBER

Halloween
Holiday, Republic of Ireland

Monday 31

First quarter
All Saints' Day

Tuesday 1

Wednesday 2

Thursday 3

Friday 4

Guy Fawkes Night

Saturday 5

Sunday 6

NOVEMBER

7 *Monday*

8 *Tuesday*

Full moon

9 *Wednesday*

10 *Thursday*

11 *Friday*

Holiday, USA (Veterans Day)
Holiday, Canada (Remembrance Day)

12 *Saturday*

13 *Sunday*

Remembrance Sunday

Merveille du jour moth *(Griposia aprilina)*

NOVEMBER

Monday **14**

Tuesday **15**

Last quarter

Wednesday **16**

Thursday **17**

Friday **18**

Saturday **19**

Sunday **20**

Tawny owl *(Strix aluco)*

NOVEMBER

21 *Monday*

22 *Tuesday*

23 *Wednesday*   *New moon*

24 *Thursday*   Holiday, USA (Thanksgiving)

25 *Friday*

26 *Saturday*

27 *Sunday*   First Sunday in Advent

Great spotted woodpecker *(Dendrocopos major)*

'Planting a single tree provides a habitat for a wide variety of insects and other animals'

INSECTS

- Butterflies and moths overwinter in places that are sheltered from wind, frost and rain. They prefer a habitat of evergreen plants and thick tangles of leaves and stems, so either plant shrubs to encourage them or give yourself a break from pruning. Some will also use garden sheds and garages so take care if you are having a clear out.
- Planting a single tree provides a host of habitats for a wide variety of insects and other animals. Look for trees with added wildlife interest such as ornamental cherries with spring blossom or rowan trees with autumn berries. Also be sure to select a tree that is right for your garden as some can get very big.

JOBS FOR THE MONTH

- Keep the bird bath topped up, clean and ice-free.
- Top up bird feeders and put food out on the ground and bird tables. Try to maintain a regular feeding regime, as this will encourage birds to return.
- Mulch vegetable beds with garden compost but delay cutting back borders until late winter to provide shelter for insects.
- Plant hedges, single-flowered roses and fruit trees to offer lots of resources for wildlife, including blossom and fruit.

CHRISTMAS DECORATIONS

Make a wildlife-friendly Christmas wreath for your front door out of garden moss, holly and ivy. If the berries have already been eaten by birds, wire in some crab apples to the wreath instead.

NOVEMBER & DECEMBER

Monday 28

Tuesday 29

First quarter
St Andrew's Day

Wednesday 30

Thursday 1

Friday 2

Saturday 3

Sunday 4

DECEMBER

---

5 *Monday*

---

6 *Tuesday*

---

7 *Wednesday*

---

8 *Thursday*   *Full moon*

---

9 *Friday*

---

10 *Saturday*

---

11 *Sunday*

Blackbird *(Turdus merula)*

DECEMBER

Monday **12**

Tuesday **13**

Wednesday **14**

Thursday **15**

Last quarter
Friday **16**

Saturday **17**

Hannukah begins (at sunset)
Sunday **18**

European hedgehog *(Erinaceus europaeus)*

DECEMBER

19 *Monday*

20 *Tuesday*

21 *Wednesday* — Winter Solstice (Winter begins)

22 *Thursday*

23 *Friday* — *New moon*

24 *Saturday* — Christmas Eve

25 *Sunday* — Christmas Day

European robin *(Erithacus rubecula)*

DECEMBER & JANUARY

Boxing Day (St Stephen's Day)
Holiday, UK, Republic of Ireland, USA,
Canada, Australia and New Zealand
Hannukah ends

Monday 26

Holiday, UK, Republic of Ireland, USA,
Canada, Australia and New Zealand (Christmas Day)

Tuesday 27

Wednesday 28

Thursday 29

First quarter

Friday 30

New Year's Eve

Saturday 31

New Year's Day

Sunday 1

Tawny owl *(Strix aluco)*

YEAR PLANNER

JANUARY	JULY
FEBRUARY	AUGUST
MARCH	SEPTEMBER
APRIL	OCTOBER
MAY	NOVEMBER
JUNE	DECEMBER